Ask the Bloody Horse

Ask the Bloody Horse

Dannie Abse

Hutchinson
London Melbourne Auckland Johannesburg

First published in Great Britain in 1986 by Century Hutchinson
Ltd, Brookmount House, 62–65 Chandos Place, Covent Garden,
London WC2N 4NW

Century Hutchinson Publishing Group (Australia) Pty Ltd
16–22 Church Street, Hawthorn, Melbourne, Victoria 3122

Century Hutchinson (NZ) Ltd
32–34 View Road, PO Box 40-086, Glenfield, Auckland 10

Century Hutchinson Group (SA) Pty Ltd
PO Box 337, Bergvlei 2012, South Africa

Set in VIP Bembo by
D. P. Media Ltd, Hitchin, Hertfordshire

Printed and bound in Great Britain by
Anchor Brendon Ltd, Tiptree, Essex

ISBN 0 09 163971 9

Acknowledgements are owed to the editors of: *Acumen*, *The American Poetry Review*, *Aquarius*, *Arc* (Canada), *Argo*, *Country Life*, *Encounter*, *The Georgia Review*, *The Jewish Chronicle*, *The Observer*, *Orbis*, *Outposts*, PEN New Poetry I, *Poetry Australia*, *Poetry Book Society Supplement 1982*, *Poetry* (Chicago), *Poetry Review*, *Poetry Wales*, *Present Tense* (USA), and *Thames Poetry*, where poems in this volume appeared during the years 1981–1985. Two earlier poems – 'The Abandoned' and 'Flowers' – have been recently revised.

Poems

Flowers

For the summer, I had prepared myself for the
    summer,
planted summer flowers to welcome friends in my
    garden.
I hoped for such a display of colour in the summer.

Into my garden a statue trespassed into my garden.
A dream! Crazed, he ordered me to turn the black
    earth over,
saying only black flowers would ever grow in my
    garden.

Now summer has come and not one black flower has
    come
out of the stone-repudiated earth of my garden –
not one flower so much in mourning that friends will
    not come.

And yet, beloved, are these but funeral flowers in my
    garden?
Their colours disguising grief that visitors cannot see?
At midnight, candidly black flowers in my garden?

Phew!

Do you know that Sumerian proverb
'A man's wife is his destiny'?
But supposing you'd been here,
this most strange of meeting places,
5000 years too early? Or me,
a fraction of a century too late?
No angel with SF wings
would have beckoned,
'This way, madam, this way, sir.'

Have you ever, at a beach,
aimed one small pebble
at another, thrown high, higher?

And though what ends
happily
is never the end,
and though the secret is
there's another secret always,

because this, because that,
because on high the Blessed
were playing ring-a-ring-o'-roses,
because millions of miles below,
during the Rasoumovsky,
the cellist, pizzicati,
played a comic, wrong note,
you looked to the right, luckily,
I looked to the left, luckily.

10

Music

Music in the beginning, before the word,
    voyaging of the spheres, their falling transport.
Like phoenix utterance, what Pythagoras heard;
    first hallucinogen, ritual's afterthought.

A place on no map. Hubbub behind high walls
    of Heaven – its bugged secrets filtering out:
numinous hauntings; sacerdotal mating-calls;
    decorous deliriums; an angel's shout.

If God's propaganda, then Devil's disgust,
    plainchant or symphony, carol or fugue;
King Saul's solace, St Cecilia's drug;
    silence's hiding-place – like sunbeams' dust.

Sorrow's aggrandizements more plangent than
    sweet;
    the soul made audible, Time's other beat.

A scream

That scream from the street erased all content,
that uninspired cry of lunacy
left a vacuum. The ears of our cat

like clown-hats lifted. And silence extended
till this room, at midnight, resumed with one
manic bluebottle tap-tapping the lampshade.

Then you, brave, concerned, pulled the curtains
   back.
We saw only the emptiness of our street
in lamplight. No blind hunter stumbled by

four times the size of a man. So many
enigmas! That night I dreamt we opened
the little wooden boxes of spikenard,

frankincense, cinnamon, saffron and myrrh;
also that herb from which can rise the antique
S-shaped, slate-coloured smoke to Paradise.

Ceilings

Sleepless, on the bed supine, I wonder
what cranky tenant left this ceiling scorched?
He must have been a giant with a flat iron.
Once, seemingly benign, another ceiling,
fifty shuffled years ago. Under it,
    my mother taught me my name,
    my father taught me the time.

Past bed-time though, poltergeists hurled lights
    outside,
caused cracks and stains to crawl, go wild, shake
    loose,
and fall malignantly beside a child
who half-awake, half beneath the bedclothes cried.
The alarm-clock hopped around the room surprised,
    flowers of the wallpaper
    poured forth illicit perfume.

The horror and the fragrance! Even at home
one may become an astonished tourist.
Listen: the oracle and the scalpelled
shadow, mumblings on the landing, almost heard.
Still emissaries from the other world
    seem near but not quite manifest,
    nag the mind like a mislaid word.

A grown man, though, should not rest so menaced,
so two-eyed, in the slow-pacing cuckoo night
of mid-summer, under a whipped ceiling,
to stare and stare again, suspiciously,
as in a zoo, at each primordial
    four-legged stain and serpent-crack
    as now I absurdly do.

Horse

You can't quite
identify it
the long straight road
unsignposted
zipping between hedges
to a scandalously
gorgeous sunset.
As you look closer
shading your eyes
with your right hand
vigilant you'll see
the visitant
the white horse
half way down it.

Do you remember?
Your father drove the car
the family squabbling
this way years ago
many a time
this Roman road
that's empty now
but for the distant
truant pink horse
with a barely
visible
red shadow
racing towards
the signals of sunset.

War-high in the sky
vapour trails fatten
and you know again
the common sense
of déjà vu. Perhaps
someone far from home
should be playing
a mouth organ
a melody slow
and sad and wanton
a tune you've heard
but can't quite say
as the purple horse
surprises the sunset.

And you close your eyes
trying to name it all.
But you recall only
the day's small prose
certain queachy things
what the office said
what the office did
as the sunset goes
as the black horse goes
into the darkness.
And you forget
how from the skin
below your thumbnail
your own moon rises.

16

Hotel nights

In the Angel Hotel

In the Angel Hotel no images allowed,
no idols. Artists, leave before midnight!

Do not strike a match in the dark laboratories
of Sleep where tomorrows are programmed.

Do not dream of stone shapes or listen to stone's
unauthorized version of silence.

Names have destinies. Write your own. Do not forge
a known sculptor's in Sleep's Visiting Book.

Else boulders will crash down. Like wood, malice of
    stone:
wood once took revenge on a carpenter's son.

Now read the instructions in the event of fire.
Note the nearest exit door. Sleep well.

In the Royal Hotel

Should you wake in the dead middle of night
to skirt-like shufflings, unearthly laughter

in the next room, pipes insistently knocking;
should there be a mouse on the next pillow,

large as a frog, or should there be a frog,
do not telephone the old night-porter.

He needs his sleep, too. Instead recall
Sheba's meeting with the king, how she journeyed

years to hear Solomon's reputed wisdom;
how she sojourned in tents without air-conditioning,

without those other extras this hotel provides –
colour TV, Radio 2, herb-foam bath fluids, etc. –

how she arrived, at last, to record his first wise
   words,
changed into her jewelled apparel, unaware

three glass walls surrounded his golden throne;
how she thought the reflections to be water,

raised her skirts daintily, regally approached.
Then the great king uttered, 'You have hairy legs.'

In the Holiday Inn

After the party I returned to the hotel.
The room was too hot so I took off my coat.

It was January but I turned down the thermostat.
I took off my shirt but I was still too hot.

I opened the window, it was snowing outside.
Despite all this the air began to simmer.

The room had a pyrexia of unknown origin.
I took off my trousers, I took off my shorts.

This room was a cauldron, this room was tropical.
On the wall, the picture of willows changed

to palm trees. In the mirror I could see the desert.
I stood naked in my socks and juggled

with pomegranates. I offered offerings
that soon became burnt. This was some holiday.

I took off one sock and read the bible.
They were cremating idols, sacrificing oxen.

I could feel the heat of their fiery furnace.
I could hear those pyromaniacs chanting.

I could smell the singed wings of cherubim.
I took off the other sock and began to dance.

Like sand the carpet scalded my twinkling feet.
Steam was coming out of both my ears.

I was King David dancing before the Lord.
Outside it was snowing but inside it was Israel.

I danced six cubits this way, six cubits that.
Now at dawn I'm hotter than the spices of Sheba.

What shall I do? I shall ask my wise son,
Solomon. Where are you Solomon?

You are not yet born, you do not know
how wise you are or that I'm your father

and that I'm dancing and dancing.

The merry-go-round at night

The roof turns, the brassy merry-go-round crashes
   out music. Gaudy horses gallop tail to snout,
   inhabit the phantasmagoria of light
   substantial as smoke. Then each one vanishes.

Some pull carriages. Some children, frightened, hold
     tight
   the reins as they arrive and disappear
   chased by a scarlet lion that seems to sneer
   not snarl. And here's a unicorn painted white.

Look! From another world this strange, lit retinue.
   A boy on a steer, whooping, loud as dynamite –
   a sheriff, no doubt, though dressed in sailor-blue.
   And here comes the unicorn painted white.

Faster! The children spellbound, the animals prance,
   and this is happiness, this no-man's land
   where nothing's forbidden. And hardly a glance
   at parents who smile, who *think* they understand

   as the scarlet lion leaps into the night
   and here comes the unicorn painted white.

(A variation of Rilke's 'Das Karussell')

Crepuscolo

*Crepuscolo (Evening) is one of the partly finished statues
by Michelangelo in the Medici Chapel, San Lorenzo.*

To the grey Sacristy of San Lorenzo
tourists come whispering lest they waken
this self-absorbed statue and it assail
each prying one of them, lest a stone hand
uplift to point and the stone head utter,
slowly turning, 'Wrongdoing and shame prevail!'

Once all drowsy in Carrara. Harmlessly,
unnumbered shadows brooded under the weight
of rock-ledges, lizards hardly animate.
Then certain men came. Still the stone's cry
safe and soundless, still the statue slumbered
in the refuge of the rock's estate.

But, soon, massive slabs were brutally urged
from the mountain – the half-bright, half-stripped bodies
of workmen struggling in dazzle and bone-
white powder of marble, smoking sunlight.
How could they discern the one waking there
or hear stone words in the larynx of the stone?

And later, in Florence? Only the sculptor
heard the statue, almost delivered, crying
'Dear to me is sleep, dearer to be at peace,
in stone, while wrongdoing and shame prevail.
Not to see, not to know, would be a great blessing.'
So the statue pleaded, so the sculptor ceased.

More than four hundred years since they set out
from Carrara, each mile cursed and supervised.
The body in the rock staying young but the hair
turning grey and the face ageing utterly –
its idioplasm fixed, its night-accepting look
despairingly defined in the eyes not there.

Now, this evening, on exercise, three warplanes
dive on Carrara, flee, return, rehearse
radioactive speeds so shamelessly
that, in the x-rayed mountain, another
fifty million statues cower, unhatched,
and not one, stone-enslaved, wanting to be free.

AWOL

Did that spy, that wax golem
in Madame Tussaud's, blink?
Above inverted Kew Bridge
which semblant swan hid
both its beaky heads
under water like a fugitive?

Abruptly tipped off by MI5,
what spirits vacated the fountains
of Trafalgar Square, quit
the fussy trees in Hyde Park?
Who, in Harley St, requested
a prescription for ambrosia?

To answer – Sssh! Sssh! –
is to listen for bare feet
traversing the carpet of a hall;
to hear, in an evening room,
one small needle wakening
a Schubert piano sonata.

Listen, you semeiologists!
It's the code of nightfall:
some lit windows, some dark;
fingers without fingerprints;
palms unlined. Forgery
in the sky, fire in the garden.

As if the Dii Majores joked
he was somewhere in London,
one of the sempiternal
30,000, unknown gods
who, after the annual feast,
visibly disappeared: smoke.

Millie's date

With sedative voices we joke and spar
as white coats struggle around her bed.
Millie's 102, all skull; once her head
was lovely – eyes serious, lips ready to be kissed
at Brixham, in 'the County of Heaven'.
She's outlived three wars and three husbands.
Her only child 'passed over', aged 77.

Sometimes she plucks the life-line in her small
left hand; remarks, 'An itch means money.'
Mostly, though, she's glum or incontinent
with memories. But now, like that immortal
of Cumae who hung in a jar, she cries,
'Let me die, let me die,' – silencing us.
How should we reply? With unfunny science?

Or, 'Not to worry – the Angels of Death
survive forever'? Often I've wondered
if some are disguised as vagrants, assigned
to each of us and programmed to arrive
punctually for their seedy appointments.
So where's Millie's escort, in which doss-house?
Has he lost his way, has he lost his mind?

Millie's quiet now, in a valium doze,
and window by window the building darkens
as lights go home. Outside, I half-expect
a doss-house beggar with a violin
to play, 'Ah, sweet mystery of Life' – some song
like that. Then any passer-by could drop
two coins, as big as eyes, inside his hat.

Case history

'Most Welshmen are worthless,
an inferior breed, doctor.'
He did not know I was Welsh.
Then he praised the architects
of the German death-camps –
did not know I was a Jew.
He called liberals, 'White blacks',
and continued to invent curses.

When I palpated his liver
I felt the soft liver of Goering;
when I lifted my stethoscope
I heard the heartbeats of Himmler;
when I read his encephalograph
I thought, '*Sieg heil, mein Fuhrer.*'

In the clinic's dispensary
red berry of black bryony,
cowbane, deadly nightshade, deathcap.
Yet I prescribed for him
as if he were my brother.

Later that night I must have slept
on my arm: momentarily
my right hand lost its cunning.

The sacred disease

In another century, a wide-eyed priest
would be at Mr Kramer's ear: 'Gaspar
bears the myrrh, Melchior the frankincense,
Balthazar the gold. Go, spirit, depart.'
Else some old quack, a colleague in my art,
would prescribe blood of a red-haired woman,
young vulture's brain, young cormorant's heart.

When God entered Paradise, all the trees
burst into hymns; but here, on earth, demons
thrived, some unquiet, trapped in skulls. How odd
Guainerius's advice: 'Doctor of brainstorm,
or of dancing mania, should you see
your wincing patient fall, then urinate
in your shoe and let him drink it while it's warm.'

Greeks with Falling Sickness were less possessed
by demons than by gods. And what of
Saul's aura, Paul's faint? I think Kramer screamed
as loud, gnashed his teeth, rolled his eyes alight,
heavenward – like any agitated saint.
Comes night, they say, most epileptics pray.
Well, once, black fire wrote aleph on the white.

Today, the Supernatural's been converted
(and all its staff) into electrical
discharges. Read the encephalograph!
Mr Kramer, though, rises now dismayed.
Whom did he visit? He feels his skull with care
as if to find it trephined, some hole there
primeval, the secret spirit betrayed.

Tuberculosis

Not wishing to pronounce the taboo word
I used to write, 'Acid-fast organisms.'
Earlier physicians noted with a quill,
'The animalcules generate their own kind
and kill.' Some lied. Or murmured, 'Phthisis,
King's Evil, Consumption, Koch's Disease.'
But friend of student days, John Roberts, clowned,
'TB I've got. You know what TB signifies?
Totally buggered.' He laughed. His sister cried.
The music of sound is the sound of music.

And what of that other medical student,
that other John, coughing up redness on
a white sheet? 'Bring me the candle, Brown.
That is arterial blood, I cannot be deceived
in that colour. It is my death warrant.'
The cruelty of Diseases! This one, too.
For three centuries, in London, the slow, sad bell.
Helplessly, wide-eyed, one in five died of it.
Doctors prescribed, 'Horse-riding, sir, ride and ride.'
Or diets, rest, mountain air, sea-voyages.

Today, an x-ray on this oblong light
clear that was not clear. No pneumothorax,
no deforming thoracoplasty. No flaw.
The patient nods, accepts it as his right
and is right. Later, alone, I, questing for
old case-histories, open the tight desk-drawer
to smell again Schiller's rotten apples.

In the old age home where he says he's resting

he tree-watches, this autumn, zany Prospero,
ex-stage magician, old star of the lost Empires,
at the window, his powdered face perfect gallows.

Look our own eidolon! Between daft paragraphs
he hums 'Daisy, Daisy,' chuckles mildewed jokes
and waits for condescending visitors to laugh.

Like that tree, his mind's half ruined. Again
    complains
but not of Caliban: 'Son, any child could tell
this place needs renovating, can't you smell the
    drains?'

Or grumbles: 'Any child could tell they steal my
    clothes;'
suspects the Superintendent's snazzy shirt is his
before switching off to a mouth-gaping doze,

to the bleak mechanism. How molesting it
always is, the last real act. Does Miranda neglect him
now he cannot summon music from the Pit?

Prospero snores on. Ariel is unconfined, free,
and any child could tell but none will tell the child,
'Tis magic, magic, that hath ravished thee.'

A salute on the way
(*To Peter Porter*)

In the Land of late Evening,
miles yet from the bus terminus
where the electric outskirts end
abruptly (far beyond, the Old
Management is about to mend
    the fused stars) I hear you laugh.
    A warm, democratic laugh.

But I remember your 'Alas'
when the needle played the 'sssh' of black
round and round the record's label.
Then the god's thesmothete decreed
(all his aces on the table)
    the game was over – your bill
    the cost of seriousness.

It seems you've often played the lead
in a tragedy translated
by a too cheerful Australian
where the hero, at home, bereaved,
alone and feeling alien,
    takes off unscripted glasses
    quietly, to rub his eyes.

Thus, in the Land of late Evening,
though I hear, now, your candid laugh
more generous than a bridegroom's,
I can guess how, afterwards, you,
like good St Peter, will resume
    the slightly-pained look of one
    about to be crucified

upside-down. Peter-come-lately,
it's your turn to complain of
a *Collected Poems*; of rust
in the morning pelvis; of teeth
touching; of colleagues become dust;
    and nothing to say except
    facts, cats, and thriving heartache,

or who pushed whom and which one fell
(that yellow stain *is* Humpty Dumpty)
so to hell with the Old Management's
jackal-headed, hired psychopomp
whispering of money unspent,
    out there, in the banked darkness:
    'Follow me, follow, follow.'

Friend, let's not hurry. Who believes
these days in a second edition?
May we, unremaindered, go slow,
shadows lengthening between lampposts
on leafy pavements, or on snow,
   to the very last lamppost
   in the Land of late Evening.

In the Pelican

As a car rushes beneath a railway bridge
and its radio suffers local amnesia
so I'm also afflicted excuse me is that
YOUR glass so sorry with sudden blanks for
    instance
I've forgotten her name so how can I phone her
look her up in the book though last time in April
when I drove her home February actually
she was an ace she really was I remembered
to remember a mnemonic that would help me
to remember and now I've forgotten THAT
except it had something to do with the colour
of her dress which matched absolutely spot on
the audacious violet colour of her eyes and
YES this should interest you I made the mnemonic
rhyme with one of the old songs the really old songs
like Stormy Weather only it wasn't Stormy
Weather it wasn't Everybody's Doing It
it wasn't Smoke Gets in Your Eyes not Lazybones
not Stardust not Shoe-shine Boy not Whispering
    Grass
not it's on the tip of my tongue or was it
Thanks for the Memory you know what's his name
used to sing it in tandem with anyway
she was SO desirable and hell I wish I'd
asked her sorry Freud would certainly say something
stupid about how I keep reaching for your glass

A welcome in the wolds

Superior people never make long visits.
                              Marianne Moore

First day, Welcome! Welcome! We even ask your
pet centaur – such a sweetie – if he'd like a bed or a
stable
  WOULD YOU LIKE A BED OR A STABLE?

First week, we offer you a symphony for a song, a
garden for a daisy. We live to give. You wake to take.

Second week, we are *exhausted* with giving.
Breakfast lunch tea dinner. So much shopping, so
much cooking, so much serving and clearing up. So a
treat, perhaps, at our favourite restaurant?
  Your centaur eats like a horse. You *almost* insist on
paying.
  This is the beginning of But. This is the beginning
of We don't mind. This is the beginning of Course
not, silly.

Next day your centaur leaves our loo in one helluva
spectacular mess.
  Forget it, silly. Forget *it*.

And next week the conclusion of But. For the
foisty centaur phones a friend on Mount Pindus, then
one in the forests of Thessaly, then another in
Famagusta and yet another in *Inner* Mongolia.
  For hours.
  Naturally he eats the last straw.
  So you're for it sweetheart – you and your
phone-mad, full-bottomed, self-centred centaur.

Your finger for a fingernail, your eye for an
eyelash.

No matter, when you depart you're smiling, when
you depart we're smiling. Goodbye!
(In the hall, we pretend not to hear your centaur
farting.)
Goodbye!
Such a shame you both can't stay,
such a shame your pet must see
his Jungian Analyst.
Goodbye! Goodbye!

Now in the stable – renamed the Hercules Room –
a new sign: NO CENTAURS ALLOWED, NO
NEMEAN LIONS, NO LERNEAN HYDRA,
NO ARCADIAN STAGS, NO
ERYMANTHIAN BOARS, NO CRETAN
BULLS, NO CANNIBAL BIRDS, NO
THREE-HEADED DOGS, ETCETERA,
ETCETERA.

And in our guest-room a little card, beautifully
printed and framed on the wall: YOUR VISIT
GIVES US SO MUCH PLEASURE, IF NOT
YOUR ARRIVAL THEN YOUR
DEPARTURE.

A translation from the Martian
(*For Craig Raine*)

Who for the first time on earth saw the object that
earth-men call an and-mirror (sic)
  who incognito picked it up who stared at it whose
eyes widened whose sixth toe curled up
  who cried out delightedly
    'Father. Father.'

Who hid it in his pocket who concealed the object
where his long-dead father lived
  who occasionally gazed at it
  who smiled at it sweetly who spoke to it softly
    'Father. Father.'

Who returned home with it who kept his hand
upon his pocket who did not show the ghost to his
wife
  who became suspicious who came close to smell
him who waited for his sixth toe to fall asleep who
stole the object from his pocket who secretly stared at
it who cried out scornfully
    'Ach. It's only an old woman.'

Who took it to the window who watched it fall in
slow-motion who heard it clatter an hour later
on the red-hard rocks below
  where the and-mirror (sic) broke into moonlight.

Watching a woman putting on lipstick

Last night the winds of May, the winds of May.
This morning the ruffled cherry blossom
has thrown its reflection to the pavement
so that it can see itself.

Pathetic fallacies

My dear one is mine as mirrors are lonely
                          W. H. Auden

Afternoon mirror

So vain that mirror on the wall.
It waits there and waits there
just to be looked at.

Evening mirror

Lonely, wishes another mirror
could be brought in, close by, opposite,
that it may reproduce itself.

Night-time mirror

Suffers from nyctalopia, panics.
Depth charges to its surface. Sleepless,
prays to its own ghost, the window.

Morning mirror

At last, at last, Visiting Hour.
The portrait gallery is open.
The Director does not seem pleased.

Quests

To reach the other world some sought hemlock
in waste-places: umbels of that small white flower
   still sway at eye-level when the eye is still;

and some, at broad sunset, walked the sea-shore
or prayed for their messiah in a darkening house.
   But gods had human faces and were flawed.

When prying Apion, with eerie conch,
summoned Homer's spirit to ask where he was born
   whose bloody head appeared above the parapet?

Now at this seaport, in its shut museum,
a sculptured satyr on a sculptured sea-horse
   blows only silent zeros through his horn.

And here, out of doors, more abundant silence.
Awesome over the sea, from which no sulking
   Proteus
   will rise, the candled stars, the unblinking moon.

Who knows? Not me. Secular, I'll never hear
the spheres, their perfect orchestra, or below,
   with joy, old Triton playing out of tune.

The message

Found in the ruin
this urgent message:
I beg you, kindle
the fire I've prepared
in the secret forest.
Then say the old prayer.

But who can locate
that clandestine forest?
Under which tall tree
should the small fire blaze?
Besides, who can recall
the old words of the prayer?

No matter. Beautiful
the yellowing scroll,
its wild imperative,
its holy message,
that we shall keep safe
in safe or museum.

The vow

I dreamt or read on a yellowing page
how the wise one rode into Chezib's shade
   and a man shouted angrily,
    'Rabbi, nullify my vow!'

Didn't the sage turn to the man's companions
(some short, some tall, some grinning, some afraid)
   to cry, 'What? Is he drunk? Has he
   swallowed half a lug of wine?'

For three miles the man stumbled, zig-zagging
behind the ass, till the bearded one dismayed,
   dismounted, wrapped himself, sat
   with knees splayed on the dark grit.

Slow lessons of sunset. The man waited,
the ass waited also. The rabbi swayed
   with a ghost-wasp in his throat;
   at first star, nullified the vow.

This I recall from so many erasures.
Now dust falls on ledges, thousands of years fade;
   but listen, the crowds shout again.
   Look! The goggled outriders!

And behind the linked arms of policemen
I clutch, as beflagged cars cavalcade,
   a half lug of wine to wonder
   what was my vow, what was his vow?

The abandoned

There is no space unoccupied by the Shekinah
                                    Talmud

. . . thy absence doth excel
All distance known
                    George Herbert

1

God, when You came to our house
    we let You in. Hunted,
        we gave You succour,
            bandaged Your hands,
                bathed Your feet.

Wanting water we gave You wine.
Wanting bread we gave You meat.

Sometimes, God, You should recall
    we are Your hiding-place.
        Take away these hands
            and You would fall.

Outside, the afflicted pass.
    We only have to call.
        They would open You
            with crutch and glass.

Who else then could we betray
   if not You, the nearest?
      God, how You watch us
        and shrink away.

2

Dear God in the end you had to go.
Dismissing you, your absence made us sane.
We keep the bread and wine for show.

The white horse galloped across the snow,
melted, leaving no hoofmarks in the rain.
Dear God, in the end, you had to go.

The winds of war and derelictions blow,
howling across the radioactive plain.
We keep the bread and wine for show.

Sometimes what we do not know we know –
who can count the stars, call each one by name?
Dear God in the end you had to go.

Yet boarding the last ship out all sorrow
that grape is but grape and grain is grain.
We keep the bread and wine for show.

Soon night will be like feathers of the crow,
small lights upon the shore begin to wane.
Dear God in the end you had to go,
we keep the bread and wine for show.

Horizon

From these outskirts of Beersheba
a car moved away leaving a dream:
the surprise of a camel standing there.

At this garage, a bored camel beside
three dirty-coloured petrol pumps.
All day I wished I'd had a camera.

Suddenly, the camel's owner appeared,
solitary, melanous, centuries old.
Had he once climbed out of a corpse?

Proximate, the appalling and the appealing.
Even here, among flies, oil-drums, vacuum-
dust, advertisements, one of the 36?

The camel, disdainful, but scaled without fuss.
No word, no farewell. Half asleep I stayed
to watch them for miles becoming smaller, small.

Over the Negev, at last, the sun tired,
honey and thorns; still I could see
near the horizon, the suggestion of

a smudge moving. Which way? A return?
The apparelled rider on his camel
coming or going, going or coming?

Encounter at a Greyhound bus station

If belief, like heaven, lies beyond the facts
what serpent flies with an ant between its teeth?

asked the over-bearded man with closed eyes.
Who are they who descend when they ascend?

this kabbalist with eyes closed, asked.
Are all men in disguise except those crying?

And what exists in a tree that doesn't exist,
its eggs looted by creatures not yet created?

        ★   ★   ★   ★

Partial to paradoxes, disliking riddles,
I hummed and I hawed, I advocated

the secrets of lucidity. Then said,
Some talk in their sleep, very few sing.

Abruptly, the unwashed one opened his lids,
rattled one coin inside a tin.

I looked into the splendour of his eyes
and laid my hand upon my mouth.

        ★   ★   ★   ★

Then he scoffed: You are like the deaf man
who knows nothing of music or of dance

yet blurts out, observing musicians play
and dancers dance – Stupid, how stupid

those who carve the air this way and that,
who blow out their cheeks and make them fat,

who mill about, clutch and maul each other
as if the very earth and all would fall.

*　　*　　*　　*

And what could I, secular, say to that?
That I'm deaf to God but not in combat?

Cool pretensions of reason he'd dismiss
and if I threw stones he'd build a house.

Yet I begged: Dare to reveal, sir, not conceal;
not all, translucent, lose authority.

Fool, he replied, I'm empty, feed my tin,
which I did, of course, when the bus came in.

Exit

As my colleague prepares the syringe
(the drip flees its hour glass)
I feel the depression of Saul,
my mother's right hand grasping still,
her left hand suspiciously still,
and think – Shadow on the wall,
Nothing on the floor – of your
random, katabolic ways:

merciful sometimes, precise, but often
wild as delirium, or like a surgeon
with cataracts grievously unkind
as you are now, as you visit
this old lady – one beloved by me –
as you blunder and exit, moth-blind,
mistaking even the light
on mirrors for open windows;

and as my colleague prepares the syringe
I remember another butchering –
a botched suicide in a circumspect
bed-sitting room, a barely
discernible fake of a girl-corpse,
a marmoreal stillness perfect
except for the closed
plum-skin eyelids trembling;

and as my colleague prepares the syringe
I picture also a victim of war
near a road, a peasant left for dead,
conscious, black-tongued, long-agonized,
able to lift, as my mother can now,
at intervals, her troubled head.
And as my colleague drives the needle in
I want to know the meaning of this:

why the dark thalamus finally
can't be shut down when we sleep
with swift economy? Of that king
and his queen – David and Bathsheba –
the old parable is plain:
out of so much suffering
came forth the other child,
the wise child, the Solomon;

but what will spring from this
unredeemed, needless degradation,
this concentration camp for one?
My colleague forces the plunger down,
squeezes the temgesic out,
the fluid that will numb and stun.
'Shadow on the wall . . .' I call, 'Nothing
on the floor . . . Patron of the Arts!'

And as my colleague extracts the needle
from her vein, the temgesic acts
till the bruised exit's negotiated.
Then how victoriously
you hold the left passive hand
of the dummy in the bed
while I continue uselessly
to hold the other.

Last visit to 198 Cathedral Road

When, like a burglar, I entered after dark
the ground-floor flat, I don't know why I sat
in the dark, in my father's armchair,
or why, suddenly, with surgeon's pocket-torch
I hosed the objects of the living room
with its freakish light.

Living room, did I say? Dying room, rather.
So much dust, mother! Outraged, the awakened
empty fruit bowl; the four-legged table
in a fright; the vase that yawned hideously;
the pattern that ran up the curtain, took flight
to the long, wriggling, photophobic crack
in the ceiling.

Omnipotent, I returned them to the dark,
sat sightless in the room that was out
of breath and listened, that summer night,
to Nothing.

Not a fly the Z side of the windowpane,
not one, comforting, diminutive sound
when the silence calmed, became profound.

Friends

Since our acorn days we've been friends
   but now at this oak door
I sense you do not wish me well.
   Why so, I cannot tell.

Though red carpet and silver gong
   may welcome us within,
friend, be yourself. Give me your hand.
   Come, this is what we planned.

Bitter as coloquintida
   a green lampshade in the hall
turns the light on your face to bile.
   Friend, turn to me and smile.

I too have felt envy and rage,
   cursed this stranger or that;
with needles in wax, cast a spell,
   damned him or her to hell,

yet never a friend, no, not one
   I would still call a friend.
Now you whom I thought to be loyal
   wish me under the soil.

Apology

I have spoken so much lately
of death and of treachery,
better to have sung the forgotten
other song of Solomon.
Forgive me. I do not believe
the rainbow was invisible
till Noah saw it;
nor was I refreshed
by strange bread in the desert,
spring water in the desert.

The two drab tablets of stone
were two drab tablets of stone,
yet, beloved, this is my heritage;
also music of Solomon's song
on psaltery and dulcimer,
that which is lost but not lost —
like the beautiful rod of Aaron,
the beautiful rod of Aaron
first with its blossom
then with its ripe almonds.

Somewhere

Not because they'd chant a god up with spell,
daft bell, corybantic ceremony,
to hear him speak translated English, badly dubbed,
hardly synchronizing with his lips,

is there a closed room, somewhere, with polished
table, silver tray, glass of soap–bubbles
boiling over. Prettily, these bubbles float
in transparencies of cathedral silence.

They break on soundless objects, on chairs,
on hushed curtains, on ceiling, on walls.

Who wants one coloured bubble not to burst,
a door to open for its triumphant exit?